Inspired
by the
WOW Moments
of Life

33 LESSONS ON

- ♡ BEING PRESENT
- ♡ LETTING GO
- ♡ SELF-CARE
- ♡ STAYING POSITIVE
- ♡ MOVING FORWARD

Words of Wisdom for the Journey

Lucy Wellmaker

To my husband
Wes
for inviting me to become a
"Wellmaker".

To my children
Maria and Vince
for all that you have taught me.

To everyone
who encouraged and
inspired me to write this book.

TABLE OF CONTENTS

Chapter 1: Lessons on Being Present

Chapter 2: Lessons on Letting Go

Chapter 3: Lessons on Self-Care

Chapter 4: Lessons on Staying Positive

Chapter 5: Lessons on Moving Forward

INTRODUCTION

There is a wealth of wisdom available to everyone every day. This wisdom is here to help us and to guide us and to show us the way. It gives us the insights and the knowledge we need to affirm our actions and to discern our next steps. It always has our best interest in mind.

To access this wisdom we must pay attention to our lives and be open to receiving it. If our lives are too busy or too loud or too cluttered, we can easily miss it.

When we notice and act on the wisdom we receive, we live our lives more on purpose. We are better able to move forward on a positive path and find the kind of fulfillment and joy that makes our hearts want to sing and our souls want to dance.

Witnessing this wisdom never ceases to amaze me. I believe our life experiences are orchestrated in such a wondrous way that they provide us exactly what we need when we need it. While it shows up in many different ways, the ultimate source of all wisdom comes from our almighty and awesome God.

When I recognize these moments, it literally leaves me feeling and saying, "WOW!" I refer to these experiences as "WOW Moments".

While these moments sometimes leave me speechless and awestruck, they also inspire me with words of wisdom. In turn, these words of wisdom give us lessons to live by.

I invite you to read this book, one moment at a time. Be open to the wisdom within and to the lessons your life has for you. Trust your insights, act accordingly and may you too experience the WOW.

I wish you well on your journey.

Lucy
Well maker

CHAPTER 1:
Lessons on Being Present

- THE ULTIMATE GIFT -

Where Are You?

No one knows the hour he will come. It's true.

I was told that the repairman would arrive between 8AM and 12Noon. I was hoping to be the first stop so that I could get on about my business. Anxiously awaiting my turn, I found myself literally walking in circles.

The more time passed, the more I thought about where I needed to be. I felt myself getting more and more uptight. Knowing that this was not a healthy frame of mind, I made the decision to accept the situation. As I did, I could feel the stress melt away.

WOW...

"Be where you are, be at peace."

"Be where you are, be at peace."

Be Inspired

Questions to Ponder:

- Where in your life do you feel like you are going in circles?

- When are you in one place thinking about the need to be in another?

- What in your schedule needs to change and where do you need to practice being where you are?

Discover deeper meaning to everyday moments.

Words of Wisdom for the Journey

Right Now

A friend of mine called to tell me about her experience with hiring a "house fluffer" – someone who rearranges your home using what you already own in a way that works better for you.

She was extremely excited as she shared her experience with me. She loved the process and was thrilled with the results.

I could appreciate what she was saying because over the years I have somewhat "fluffed" my house as well. The part that I find so amazing is how, at first, I think I need something and then with a little rearranging I find that I had it all along.

WOW...

"I have everything I need."

"I have everything I need."

Be Inspired

Questions to Ponder:

- In what area of your life do you currently feel that there is something missing or something you need?

- What are some things you could rearrange in order to possibly meet this need?

- If this "need" was in your life to help you in some way, what might that reason be?

Discover deeper meaning to everyday moments.

Words of Wisdom for the Journey

This Is Sick

My husband had more than his usual business trips last month which included weekends away. I was looking forward to things settling down a bit so we could spend more time together, go places together and reconnect with one another.

When he returned home from his last trip, he brought home a bug. It was a nasty little bug that kept him home, sick for a week.

Halfway through the week, I started showing symptoms. Together we went to the doctor, shopped for our medicine and spent some sleepless nights helping each other out and reconnecting.

WOW...

"Sometimes the things that bug us the most have come to heal us in some way."

"Sometimes the things that bug us the most have come to heal us in some way."

Be Inspired

Questions to Ponder:

- What has been bugging you lately?

- What specifically do you want from the situation?

- What unexpected things are showing up to help you improve or heal this situation?

Discover deeper meaning to everyday moments.

Words of Wisdom for the Journey

The Road
to Peace

This week while I was driving to a meeting I got a flat tire. My first reaction was an appreciation that this was a meeting I was attending rather than one I was facilitating.

My second thought was, "Why did this happen and what am I to learn from it?"

The reason it happened was because when I came to a curve in the road I picked up a little too much speed, got too close to the edge and hit the curb.

Saying "I got a flat tire" didn't feel accurate. It was as if I was saying "the flat tire happened to me", when in fact, I caused it. I was reminded of the importance of taking responsibility for my actions.

As we cruise through life, we sometimes pick up a little extra speed. When we do, we must be aware of our situations and avoid the extreme edges.

WOW...

"Slow down and stay centered."

"Slow down and stay centered."

Be Inspired

Questions to Ponder:

- In what area of your life are you picking up too much speed and need to slow down?

- What are the edges in your life from which you want to steer clear?

- As you take time to center yourself through a few deep breaths, what nugget of wisdom is coming up for you?

Discover deeper meaning to everyday moments.

Words of Wisdom for the Journey

Watch This

When I was young and my family gathered around to watch a TV show I would often turn my back to the TV and watch my family instead. It was more interesting for me to watch them then it was to watch the show.

Years later I found myself in a similar situation, watching my children watch TV. I was mesmerized by their expressions and more so by how much they have grown and changed.

I became overwhelmed with joy as I reminisced about doing this as a child and now doing it with my own children.

WOW...

"Take time to focus on what is important to you."

"Take time to focus on what is important to you."

Be Inspired

Questions to Ponder:

- To whom/what would you like to give more of your attention?

- How can you be more present in this situation?

- What will you need to stop doing in order to focus on this more?

Discover deeper meaning to everyday moments.

Journal For Wisdom

Words of Wisdom for the Journey

You Know
What?

While my 9 year old daughter was doing her math homework, she became very frustrated. The answer to the problem that she "knew" was right just didn't seem to make sense to her.

When I suggested that the answer may be different, she disagreed. When I suggested that she trust herself and write down what she knew was right, she couldn't.

A little later, I realized why her answer was right and was able to explain it to her. It was then, that she had the confidence to write her answer down and say to me, "I told you I was right."

WOW...

"We can know things long before we really know why."

*"We can know things long before
we really know why."*

Be Inspired

Questions to Ponder:

- When did you just "know" something without really understanding how you knew it?

- How willing are you to act on a "knowing" even when it doesn't seem to make sense to do so?

- When you think about a situation that you have been trying to solve, what do you just "know" to be true about the solution?

Discover deeper meaning to everyday moments.

Words of Wisdom for the Journey

A Surprise Gift

"A package" my husband explained, will soon be arriving in the mail."

Eagerly anticipating that he was creatively keeping my Christmas gift a surprise, I listened intently grinning from ear to ear.

"When it arrives," he said. "Just wrap it and give it to me for Christmas."

My smile faded, a few things went through my mind and a couple of things came out of my mouth. Then, I remembered the intention I set to keep Christmas simple. My husband had picked out, ordered and purchased his own gift. How much simpler could it get?

WOW...

"Sometimes life delivers our intentions packaged in ways we would never expect."

"Sometimes life delivers our intentions packaged in ways we would never expect."

Be Inspired

Questions to Ponder:

- What unexpected thing has shown up in your life recently?

- In what ways could this possibly be a result of an intention you set for yourself?

- What new intentions do you now want to set for yourself?

Discover deeper meaning to everyday moments.

Journal for Wisdom

Words of Wisdom for the Journey

CHAPTER 2:
Lessons on Letting Go

- RELEASE TO RECEIVE -

Get This Straight

My hair is naturally curly and I often spend time straightening it out. With the forecast full of rain last week, I decided not to fight Mother Nature and just go curly.

A colleague complimented me on my hair and asked what I did differently. I responded by saying, "This is what happens when I let go of trying to control it."

As I spoke these words, my thoughts went deeper. I realized how often I try to control different situations.

Sometimes things go better when we let nature run its course and we keep our hands out of the situation. Sometimes, on the other hand, it is important that we do take control.

Discerning between the two can be a "hairy" situation at times.

WOW...

"When you find yourself wanting to straighten things out, consider going with the flow."

"When you find yourself wanting to straighten things out, consider going with the flow."

Be Inspired

Questions to Ponder:

- Where in your life do you feel the need to straighten things out?

- How would it be to allow this situation to unfold on its own?

- In what area of your life are you now willing to go with the flow more because you feel it would be best to do so?

Discover deeper meaning to everyday moments.

Words of Wisdom for the Journey

Enjoy
the Ride

I often hear people (myself included) compare their lives to a rollercoaster. It's a journey full of twists and turns, peaks and valleys, ups and downs. The idea is to figure out how to enjoy the ride along the way.

When my kids were younger I had a "roller coaster experience". We enjoyed taking them to amusement parks and as they got bigger, so did the rides. When we felt like they could handle it, we took them to Cedar Point in Sandusky, Ohio. At the time, it had one of the tallest and fastest roller coasters in the world.

While I had always enjoyed riding them, I realized that as I was getting older and they were getting bigger I had some fear to work through before I could really enjoy the ride. Through the power of prayer and positive self-talk I was able to raise my hands up and go.

...

"I surrender."

"I surrender."

Be Inspired

Questions to Ponder:

- In what area of your life are you not necessarily "enjoying the ride" so much right now?

- What worries and anxieties do you have around this area of life?

- What would it be like if you made the decision to let go of these fears, raising your hands up in praise that something bigger than yourself is actually in control?

Discover deeper meaning to everyday moments.

Words of Wisdom for the Journey

At
the Core

The winter storm came, just as predicted, and we received about 6 inches of snow. That is a lot of snow for us!

The next day, when my kids went out to play, I decided to join them. I put on several layers of clothes and headed out.

When I stepped outside I realized how brightly the sun was shining. Even though the temperature was reportedly very cold, it did not feel this way at all.

I was amazed at how warm it actually was. The information I received did not seem to be accurate.

We eventually took off our coats, hats, scarves and gloves. As we headed back home, I found myself carrying a bunch of extra stuff.

When I got inside, I was finally able to put it all down and take off even more layers. When I was done, I felt so light and free.

WOW...

"Peel back the layers and release what you no longer need."

*"Peel back the layers and release
what you no longer need."*

Be Inspired

Questions to Ponder:

- How have you added layers to the core of who you are based on potentially inaccurate information?

- How do you imagine you would feel if you were able to let go of some of the extra stuff you carry and no longer need?

- What are you willing to do to start the process of peeling back the layers? (Hint: Journal for Wisdom)

Discover deeper meaning to everyday moments.

Journal for Wisdom

Words of Wisdom for the Journey

Reap and
Sow What?

It was late in the spring, a little too late actually, and I was determined to plant some tomatoes. As I did, I thought of the juicy red tomatoes that these plants would produce and all the fun and tasty things that I would make with them.

It was close to the end of August and I had yet to pick my first tomato. My kitchen, however, had been overflowing with beautiful homegrown tomatoes. I was blessed to receive them from others who had more than they could use.

It was as if setting the intention to have homegrown tomatoes brought them to me, with very little effort on my part. We reap what we sow and we sow much through our intentions.

WOW...

"Be open to receiving the abundance."

"Be open to receiving the abundance."

Be Inspired

Questions to Ponder:

- What are you determined to do or to have?

- How will things be for you once this is achieved?

- As you open your hands to receive what is available to you, what will you need to release in the process?

Discover deeper meaning to everyday moments.

Words of Wisdom for the Journey

Imagine This

"Mom," my son said to me. "Imagine that you are in a room with no exit."

"Now," he continued. "How would you get out?"

"Hmmm," I thought as I began to contemplate my answer.

After offering several solutions, I still couldn't come up with the right answer. I finally gave up and asked, "So, how would I get out?"

My son simply stated. "Stop imagining."

WOW...

"What a simple solution to a stressful situation."

*"What a simple solution
to a stressful situation."*

Be Inspired

Questions to Ponder:

- Where in your life are you worried or stressing over an "imaginary" problem?

- How can you use your imagination in a positive way?

- Considering a current struggle you have, what story can you imagine to illustrate that it is serving you in some way?

Discover deeper meaning to everyday moments.

Words of Wisdom for the Journey

On Purpose

I was switching a load of laundry from the washer to the dryer when I realized it was time for me to take action. With a sense of determination, I took control and pulled the clear plastic film right off the control panel of the dryer.

It felt so good to do so.

That clear plastic film certainly had a purpose. It was intended to keep things looking new. After more than several years now, it was curling up around the edges and sabotaging its original intent.

The thing that I needed to let go of was very clear. It always is when we are open to seeing it.

WOW...

"Don't get stuck with things that no longer serve you."

"Don't get stuck with things that no longer serve you."

Be Inspired

Questions to Ponder:

- What are you currently holding on to that no longer serves you?

- How has this thing served its purpose in the past?

- What small step are you willing to take to release an unwanted feeling, thought or item?

Discover deeper meaning to everyday moments.

Words of Wisdom for the Journey

CHAPTER 3:
Lessons on Self-Care

- FILL YOUR OWN CUP -

Make Up
Your Mind

I was standing in front of my bathroom mirror getting ready for the day. Once again, I would reach for an almost empty bottle of foundation.

I tapped it on the bottom, tried to reach deep inside and wondered why I was expecting this to work. For days, I was trying to get what I needed from a bottle that was nearly empty.

I thought about how I do this in other areas of my life as well. How I often try to get what I need from people or places that just can't deliver. It's like going to a department store for a dozen eggs.

People can't give what they don't have. Sometimes we have to give ourselves what we wish we could get from others. When I finally decided to buy myself a new bottle of make-up, the satisfaction was priceless.

WOW...

"Getting what we need is the foundation to living a life we love."

"Getting what we need is the foundation to living a life we love."

Be Inspired

Questions to Ponder:

- Where have you been tapping into an empty supply, trying to get what you need?

- Knowing that people can't give what they do not have, who can you now see in a different light?

- What changes will you choose to make in order to get what you need?

Discover deeper meaning to everyday moments.

Words of Wisdom for the Journey

Reflect
on This

I love going into my son's room to look in his mirror. His mirror is so kind and forgiving. It reflects a taller, slender me.

Even though everything around me is a mess, I somehow seem to lose sight of it all. I leave his room feeling uplifted.

As I pondered this more, I realized the power that lies in how we see ourselves. While it is important to be honest with ourselves, it is also important to treat ourselves well.

WOW...

"Look at yourself in a kind and forgiving way."

"Look at yourself in a kind and forgiving way."

Be Inspired

Questions to Ponder:

- How do you currently see yourself?

- What can you choose to forgive yourself for today?

- Speaking to yourself as you would a dear friend, what loving and kind statements can you say to uplift yourself?

Discover deeper meaning to everyday moments.

Words of Wisdom for the Journey

Avoid Burnout

One of my favorite things to do when the temperature gets cold is to sit by a fire. I love to just gaze into the flames and let my mind wander.

While doing so, I thought about how something so warm and comforting can also be so dangerous and destructive.

For me, it was a wonderful reminder of how too much of a good thing is not necessarily a good thing.

WOW...

"Everything in moderation, so you don't get burned."

"Everything in moderation,
so you don't get burned."

Be Inspired

Questions to Ponder:

- What "good thing" do you have going on that no longer feels so good?

- How has it spread to be bigger than you expected or in what other ways are you spread too thin?

- How can you best protect yourself from getting burned in this situation?

Discover deeper meaning to everyday moments.

Words of Wisdom for the Journey

Find
Some Help

I don't know if people still talk about "bad hair days",
but I do know that I still have them. In fact, until recently,
I was having them way too often.

When I stopped to think about what was going on,
I realized that for the past few weeks (maybe months)
I was trying to do it all by myself. I had been out of hair
spray. I decided to get the help I needed. When I did,
the results were both amazing and immediate.

Soon afterwards I saw my neighbor. She looked at me
wide-eyed and said, "Your hair looks great!"

I thanked her and told her how I replenished my supply
of hair spray.

WOW...

"Reach out for help and get the lift you need."

"Reach out for help and get the lift you need."

Be Inspired

Questions to Ponder:

- In what area(s) of your life are you trying to "do it all by yourself"?

- In what ways and to whom can you reach out for help?

- What new thought will you need to embrace to align with you receiving the help you need in a positive way?

Discover deeper meaning to everyday moments.

Words of Wisdom for the Journey

Saying No

There was an upcoming event that I had partnered up with a colleague to do. The closer it got, the more it didn't feel right. It seemed like a lot of work for something I wasn't very excited about. My heart was not in it and I was already looking forward to it being over.

I decided to check in with my colleague to see how it would be if we didn't move forward on this. I thought about who I might disappoint and I also thought about myself. Then, I made arrangements for us not to continue with this event.

Within a few hours I was asked to do another event— one that made my heart sing and that was much more in line with my priorities.

WOW...

"Saying 'No' to things that are not aligned with our priorities makes room for things that are."

"Saying 'No' to things that are not aligned with our priorities makes room for things that are."

Be Inspired

Questions to Ponder:

- What is really important to you at this time of your life?

- How and what will you say "No" to in order to honor your true priorities?

- When saying "No" is uncomfortable, how will you remind yourself that you and your priorities are worth it?

Discover deeper meaning to everyday moments.

Words of Wisdom for the Journey

Copy This

Some days it feels like life is about doing the drills. It starts with the morning drill, then the work drill, the after-work drill and then all the drills in between and sometimes end by crashing.

I was reminded of this when I approached a copy machine one day. I had some work to do and the copy machine was resting, needing to warm up before it would perform. After it started producing results it paused, as if to take a small break, and then it continued. Later in the day I found it partially shut down in order to conserve energy.

Warming up, taking breaks, resting, conserving energy— all done in order to produce good results and avoid crashing. What wonderful reminders to receive from a copy machine.

WOW...

"Copy the machine."

Be Inspired

Questions to Ponder:

- Where in your life are over working and feel like you might crash at times?

- What are some ways that you can approach this differently, using some tips offered by the copy machine?

- How would your life be different if you decided to take better care of yourself?

Discover deeper meaning to everyday moments.

Journal for Wisdom

Words of Wisdom for the Journey

Refuel

I was driving along, not far from home, when I saw a car on the side of the road. I stopped to ask the driver if he needed any help.

I immediately recognized him as an employee of the grocery store that I frequent. He said that he ran out of gas and would appreciate a ride to the gas station. My gut told me that this was safe and so I gladly gave him the ride.

On the way to the station, he told me how he knew he was taking a chance not to get gas sooner. He said he knew he was pushing it a bit, but thought he would make it.

As he was speaking, I thought about how many of us ride through life running close to empty. We too are taking a risk and pushing it a bit. We must find a way to fill our tank before we are completely empty.

WOW...

"Ask for help, before you need it."

"Ask for help, before you need it."

Be Inspired

Questions to Ponder:

- Where in your life are you feeling a bit depleted and pushing it a bit?

- What do you need in order to feel like your tank is full again?

- How do you plan to make this happen, before it's too late?

Discover deeper meaning to everyday moments.

Journal for Wisdom

Words of Wisdom for the Journey

CHAPTER 9:
Lessons on Staying Positive

- CHOOSE LOVE -

A Special Ingredient

I went to my kitchen to make some chicken salad and ended up with a pot of soup as well. I love it when that happens!

This gives me a great sense of accomplishment, of using my resources wisely and it nurtures my need for creativity. One step naturally led to the next.

As I stirred the soup, I thought about life. I realized that if I had been asked to make soup that day I wouldn't have thought I had what it takes. In reality, because of all the steps I had taken up until this point, I had everything I needed to make it happen. And, as fate would have it, the outcome was even grander than I could imagine.

WOW...

"The efforts we make need to simmer a while before we see the results."

*"The efforts we make need to simmer
a while before we see the results."*

Be Inspired

Questions to Ponder:

- Where in your life are you not yet seeing the results of your efforts?

- What are you saying to yourself about the reason for this?

- Trusting that things take time and speaking to yourself as you would a good friend, what can you now say to offer yourself the encouragement you need and deserve?

Discover deeper meaning to everyday moments.

Journal for Wisdom

Words of Wisdom for the Journey

The Power Within

Earlier today we lost our power. Whenever this happens I find myself thinking about what I can and can't do around the house.

I can take a shower, but I can't dry my hair. I can wash dishes, but I can't do laundry. I can dust, but I can't vacuum. And, even though I know the lights won't work, I find myself flipping the switch when I enter the room. It's a habit.

As I reflected on this, I started thinking about the power we have within us. We have the power to choose love in a hateful situation, the power to choose peace when surrounded by stress and the power to let go even when it is scary to do so.

Instead of flipping the switch, we sometimes walk around in the dark nurturing our negative emotions. Today's short power outage reminded me that the power within me is always available. It's up to me to tap into it.

WOW...

"Flip the switch and use your power."

"Flip the switch and use your power."

Be Inspired

Questions to Ponder:

- What area of your life feels a bit dark right now?

- How ready and willing are you to shed some light on this situation?

- If you tapped into the power that lies within you, how might your situation be different?

Discover deeper meaning to everyday moments.

Words of Wisdom for the Journey

Part of
the Journey

We were on the highway headed home when the stomach bug hit our family. My son indicated that he needed to get out of the van. I quickly took the exit at hand, pulled over on the side of the road and opened his door—almost just in time.

It's amazing how quickly one's journey can take a different path. Minutes before, we were cruising along and all was well. Now, we had quite a mess to deal with. We were forced to be resourceful using what we had to make the best of the situation.

Before long we were on the road again. When we got home this situation, like many others, got worse before it got better. Then, after about 24 hours later, all is well again.

WOW...

"This too shall pass."

"This too shall pass."

Be Inspired

Questions to Ponder:

- What messy situation have you had to deal with in the past?

- What lesson(s) did you learn once you got on the other side of it?

- Regarding any current challenges, what do you need to remind yourself about today?

Discover deeper meaning to everyday moments.

Words of Wisdom for the Journey

Sometimes
Life Stinks

I was noticing a bad order coming from underneath our kitchen sink. I didn't know what it was. I moved things around and cleaned things out and the odor remained.

After a while, I began to fear the worst. Could this possible have something to do with a dead animal?

A few days later when I went to take a closer look, I found an old potato that somehow was forgotten about. I was so excited to find this moldy thing.

WOW...

"Even the rotten things in life can be a blessing."

"Even the rotten things in life can be a blessing."

Be Inspired

Questions to Ponder:

- What "rotten" thing are you currently dealing with in your life?

- What good has or might come from this unpleasant situation?

- How can you make the most of this situation?

Discover deeper meaning to everyday moments.

Take Out
the Trash

Things are just not the same.

For years we have spent time on Sundays gathering up
our trash, getting it out the door and taking it to the curb.
It was a habit, part of our routine. Not anymore.

Or trash day was changed from Mondays to Tuesdays.
It's been an adjustment. It'll take some time to get used
to this.

For quite a while I found myself thinking about it
on Sundays. It took time to retrain my mind.

WOW...

"Learn to release the garbage from your mind."

"Learn to release the garbage from your mind."

Be Inspired

Questions to Ponder:

- What types of "garbage" are you in the habit of thinking about?

- What kind and loving thoughts can you use to replace these?

- What will your life be like when you are able to release the negative thinking into a more positive way of being?

Discover deeper meaning to everyday moments.

Words of Wisdom for the Journey

Time to Fly

I was speaking to someone outdoors when a butterfly
flew by. She said that it was good luck for a butterfly
to cross one's path.

Later that day, while I was driving down the highway,
a butterfly flew right into my path and crashed into my
windshield. I wasn't sure if this meant I was going to be
really lucky or if I had just ruined any chance of good luck.

Since then butterflies have continued to cross my path
in the most interesting ways. For me, they have become a
reminder of what can come out of a dark and lonely place.

WOW...

"In time, your spirit will soar."

"In time, your spirit will soar."

Be Inspired

Questions to Ponder:

- Looking back, when have you been able to come out of a "dark and lonely place"?

- What are some things or signs that help you know you will get through another such temporary phase of life?

- How is it for you when your spirit soars and life is good?

Discover deeper meaning to everyday moments.

Words of Wisdom for the Journey

CHAPTER 5:
Lessons on
Moving Forward

- BABY STEPS COUNT -

Take Action

The load I was carrying got heavier and heavier. I could feel the weight on my shoulders. I knew it was time to get rid of some stuff. It was time for me to clean out my pocketbook.

It would only take about ten minutes and yet I continued to put it off, lugging around the additional weight and clutter that caused me stress and frustration. I wasn't ready.

Then, I had a dream. I was in line to board a plane. I was fumbling through my pocketbook to find my ticket. I was becoming more and more anxious as I moved closer to the front of the line, still unable to find my ticket to board. My pocketbook was a mess. I realized that I could miss my flight because I had refused to act on what I knew I needed to do.

The next morning when I awoke, I cleaned out my pocketbook. When I was done, I felt so light and so free. It almost felt like I could fly.

WOW...

"Take Action—Take Flight."

Be Inspired

Questions to Ponder:

- What is currently weighing you down in your life?

- What small action step have you been putting off?

- How will things be for you once you take this step?

Discover deeper meaning to everyday moments.

Words of Wisdom for the Journey

Open the Door

My husband and I were sitting outside on our deck having a conversation. When we got up to go inside my husband opened the door. For no apparent reason, the handle of the storm door fell off and all the pieces dropped down.

When I stepped inside I thought about the reason this might be happening. I also thought about what we were just talking about.

Then, it all became clear. It was time to pick up the pieces.

WOW...

"Get a handle on the situation."

"Get a handle on the situation."

Be Inspired

Questions to Ponder:

- What situation do you currently need to get a handle on?

- What are the pieces of this situation that need to be addressed and handled?

- How will things look once you get past this particular situation?

Discover deeper meaning to everyday moments.

Catch This

I was throwing the football with my son and he was giving some helpful tips along the way. When we started doing the running passes he said, "Don't throw it to where I am. Throw it to where I am going."

Interesting, I thought.

Football is about moving forward to reach a goal. The same concept applies to life. It's so easy to get caught up in where we are right now and to lose sight of the big picture.

When I thought about how I could best position myself to catch my pass and reach my goal, I realized I needed to embrace the future (technology and all) rather than resist it.

WOW...

"Focus on where you're going and embrace what's coming your way."

"Focus on where you're going and embrace what's coming your way."

Be Inspired

Questions to Ponder:

- Where, in your life, do you want to be a year from now?

- What are you currently doing that might keep you stuck in the place you are now?

- What situation or challenges will you need to embrace to get where you want to be?

Discover deeper meaning to everyday moments.

Words of Wisdom for the Journey

Drill It Down

I went to the dentist for a scheduled procedure for which I was confident that I needed and wanted. As the chair was reclining back, I felt the fear set in and I began to doubt the situation.

I asked them to stop and I expressed my concerns. I received a little reassurance, but there were still a lot of unknowns for me.

What I did know was that I wanted to move forward. In that moment, I made the decision to trust.

Two hours later, after many unpleasant sights and sounds, the results were good. In time, they will be even better.

WOW...

"Trust that everything is going to be okay."

"Trust that everything is going to be okay."

Be Inspired

Questions to Ponder:

- Where are you experiencing some doubt with a situation you were once confident in?

- How confident are you in wanting to move forward with this situation?

- What would it be like if you decided to trust the process because you knew that things would work out well?

Discover deeper meaning to everyday moments.

Words of Wisdom for the Journey

Show Me the Way

I recently heard someone say that when men get lost, they rarely stop to ask for directions.

I grew up with a very different example. My dad would literally stop in the middle of the road to ask for help if he needed it.

As I reflect on this, I realize we have a similar opportunity when we feel lost with the direction of our lives. We can stop, in the middle of what we are doing, and ask for the direction we need.

Until we get a clear message of which way to go, we may need to stay right where we are.

WOW...

"Look for the signs."

"Look for the signs."

Be Inspired

Questions to Ponder:

- Where in your life could you use some direction?

- What specifically are you trying to discern?

- What messages or signs have you already received regarding this situation?

Discover deeper meaning to everyday moments.

Words of Wisdom for the Journey

The Cycle of Success

The other day I was reminded of one of my fondest memories. It was of a family vacation where my husband and I rented two tandem bikes for ourselves and our two young children.

Our children were so excited and also scared because they had not yet learned to ride a bike. At least, that is, without training wheels.

Looking at these bikes, they didn't think that they would be able to do it. To them, it seemed impossible and a bit frightening as well.

I remember telling them to trust us. All they had to do was hold on and enjoy the ride.

Once they realized we could keep them up and balanced, they could relax and help us pedal. It was so much fun.

WOW...

"Hold on and enjoy the ride."

"Hold on and enjoy the ride."

Be Inspired

Questions to Ponder:

- What in your life seems a bit scary and almost impossible to successfully do?

- Who or what can you put your trust in for the support and balance you need to be held up as you take on this challenge?

- Imagine that all you really need to do to enjoy a successful outcome is to "hold on"—what does that look like for you?

Discover deeper meaning to everyday moments.

Words of Wisdom for the Journey

Never
Lose Sight

33

While at my daughter's soccer game this past week I found myself mesmerized by the enthusiasm of one of the other moms. She was cheering our team on for every little thing they did. As she clapped and cheered she would also shout out what she saw them doing right.

As I listened and watched, I wondered if this was her natural way of being. Or maybe this was a way to give her husband, who is blind, a play by play account of what was happening.

As I continued to observe the situation, I realized that we can't always see how close we are to our goal. It's important that we acknowledge our progress along the way.

WOW...

"Celebrate every step forward."

"Celebrate every step forward."

Be Inspired

Questions to Ponder:

- What is one of your current goals in life—something that you have either consciously or even unconsciously been working towards?

- What are some ways that you have made progress in this area? (Think about the "little things" they can have great impact.)

- How can you celebrate your success thus far? (At the very least, congratulate yourself in writing.)

Discover deeper meaning to everyday moments.

Words of Wisdom for the Journey

Thank You

for allowing me to share this work with you.

If, at any moment, you were inspired while reading this book please consider gifting one to someone else to inspire them.

I wish you well,

Lucy
Well maker

It doesn't end here.

Lucy Wellmaker continues to share her "WOW Moments" on a weekly basis through her blog at www.LucyWellmaker.com

Take a moment and subscribe now.

CPSIA information can be obtained
at www.ICGtesting.com
Printed in the USA
BVHW07s1417230518
517122BV00024B/914/P